KUrt & Scott's
JUNIOR HIGH ADVENTURE

Taking Your Ministry Beyond Duct Tape,
Dodgeball & Double-Dog Dares

Kurt Johnston
Scott Rubin

Group

Incredible things will happen™

Loveland, Colorado
www.group.com

Group

Kurt and Scott's Jr. High Adventure

Copyright © 2008 Kurt Johnston and Scott Rubin

Visit our Web site: **www.group.com**

Credits

Editor: Scott M. Kinner
Senior Developer: Patty Anderson
Project Manager: Pam Clifford
Chief Creative Officer: Joani Schultz
Copy Editor: Ann Jahns
Art Director and Print Production Artist: Andrea Filer and Patricia Reinheimer
Cover Art Director/Designer: Andrea Filer
Cover Illustrator: Andrea Filer
Illustrator: Andrea Filer
Production Manager: DeAnne Lear

Library of Congress Cataloging-in-Publication Data

Johnston, Kurt, 1966-
Kurt and Scott's junior high adventure : taking your ministry beyond duct tape, dodgeball & double-dog dares / Kurt Johnston and Scott Rubin.
-- 1st American pbk. ed.
     p. cm.
ISBN 978-0-7644-3739-7 (pbk. : alk. paper) 1. Church work with teenagers. 2. Junior high school students--Religious life. I. Rubin, Scott. II. Title.
BV1475.9.J65 2008
259'.23--dc22

Printed in the United States of America.
10 9 8 7 6 5 4 3 2 1   17 16 15 14 13 12 11 10 09 08

Table of Contents

Foreword

I've been editor of GROUP Magazine for two decades—that means I've seen and edited an Everest-esque mountain of youth ministry ideas over the years. You'd think, after all that time, that I'd pretty much seen "everything under the sun." But the truth is, the longer I do this, the more I appreciate (and am surprised by) a certain kind of ministry idea or bit of mentoring advice. These are the ideas offered by youth leaders who have STS.

Now, this is going to sound a little silly…because it *actually is* kind of silly. STS is the abbreviation I use when I'm training novice writers on how to get published—it stands for Something To Say. I tell them that every editor is looking for STS, and it really doesn't matter how well you write if you don't have STS as the "payload" for your article. Always, people ask how they can get the STS I'm looking for. And I tell them it has everything to do with experience and practice and risk and failure and perseverance and insight and passion.

And that brings me to Kurt Johnston.

Kurt started writing his GROUP Magazine column on junior high ministry five or six years ago. When you're the junior high pastor at Orange County's Saddleback Church, there's a general assumption (right or wrong) that you have STS. Well, I had no idea how true that assumption would be when Kurt first started writing for GROUP. Three or four months ago, I saw Kurt and told him, "You're one of the best writers I've ever worked with at GROUP." And that means, in my STS value system, that Kurt has consistently, amazingly offered the most practical, surprising, wise, and innovative ideas for junior high ministry that I've ever seen.

So, it was a no-brainer for us to put together the best-of-the-best of what Kurt has written over the years—as a gift of STS to junior high leaders who are driven by the same passions that Kurt is driven by. But the really *great* thing about the book you're about to read is that we somehow convinced Scott Rubin, Kurt's good friend and the junior high pastor at Willow Creek Church in suburban Chicago, to "salt" his own STS into this stew of great ministry ideas. Scott, like Kurt, can draw from many years of "experience and practice and risk and failure and perseverance and insight and passion."

Together, these two guys put the STS quota over the top. You're going to like this book—you'll laugh, you'll cry, you'll be tempted to do cartwheels. Or maybe that's just me…I love it when gifted people give what they have to give. And that's what Kurt and Scott have done here.

Rick Lawrence
GROUP Magazine Executive Editor

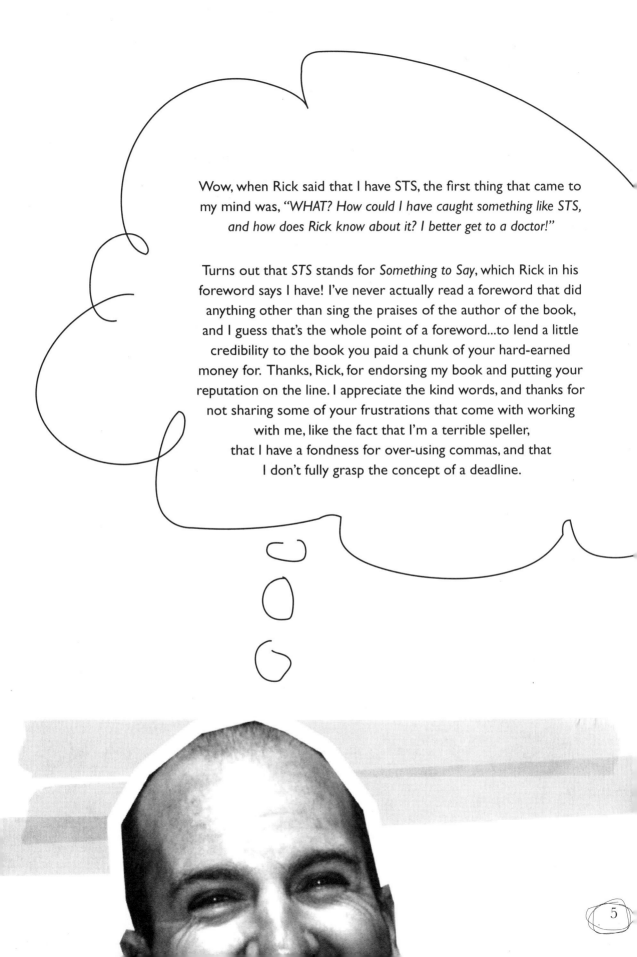

Wow, when Rick said that I have STS, the first thing that came to my mind was, *"WHAT? How could I have caught something like STS, and how does Rick know about it? I better get to a doctor!"*

Turns out that *STS* stands for *Something to Say*, which Rick in his foreword says I have! I've never actually read a foreword that did anything other than sing the praises of the author of the book, and I guess that's the whole point of a foreword...to lend a little credibility to the book you paid a chunk of your hard-earned money for. Thanks, Rick, for endorsing my book and putting your reputation on the line. I appreciate the kind words, and thanks for not sharing some of your frustrations that come with working with me, like the fact that I'm a terrible speller, that I have a fondness for over-using commas, and that I don't fully grasp the concept of a deadline.

Introduction

I think the silly title of this little book really says it all. Working with junior high students is quite an adventure. It's an adventure that I've been on since way back in 1988 and one that my friend Scott has been on since the late '90s. And it's an adventure both of us hope to continue to be a part of for years to come!

Here's how this book became a reality: I've had the joy of writing a little column for GROUP Magazine for several years. Over that time I've written about my joys, frustrations, successes, and failures. (I haven't written about *all* of my failures, because… well, because if people knew how often I failed I doubt they'd keep reading my column!) Each column has reflected my own personal journey in ministry to young teens and, I hope, has served to encourage others on a similar journey.

Not long ago the good people at Group approached me with an idea:

Group "Kurt, we have an idea."

 "Uh, OK. What is it?"

Group "We think we should bind a bunch of your best columns together and make them into a book, because lots of current junior high youth workers have probably never read them."

Kurt "I think I've only written one *good* column, so how can we possibly find enough *best* ones to make a book?"

Group "Well, maybe two. (Laughter.) We'll ask your buddy Scott to add commentary from his ministry perspective. That will help make your columns stronger and something others can really learn from."

Kurt "So you're saying Scott will add strength and practicality to my columns…I'm not sure how I'm supposed to take that."

Group (Laughter.) "Actually, we think it's a great idea that will create a dynamic resource and help lots of people who love junior high kids."

Kurt "Well, if you put it that way…"

OK, that's not exactly how the conversation went, but you get the idea. This book is a compilation of my writings over the past seven years with insights recently added from my close friend Scott Rubin. Because we're such good friends, I've given him permission to speak frankly about the stuff I wrote. There will be times he says, "Amen, brother!"— yeah right, like anybody from Willow Creek talks like that!—and times he says, "Bro, you don't know what you're talking about." Our hope is that our experiences…our adventures…in junior high ministry will combine to give you some great insight and encouragement as you minister to the students God has called you to.

May your adventure be as wonderful as ours!

Kurt Johnston

A Picture of Junior High Ministry

Kurt Before you read any further, find a pen. Now look to the end of this section. See those three little boxes? Good. You're going to need to know where they are. Look again. Are they still there? Gotcha!

First, in each box draw a little dot in the bottom left-hand corner and a little cross in the upper right-hand corner. I'll wait. Are you ready? In these three boxes you're going to draw what I believe is a picture of junior high ministry.

Scott *Oh, great—if I need to be an artist to be in junior high ministry, I'm in trouble!*

Kurt Now in the first box I want you to draw a straight line from the dot to the cross. What you have just drawn is a picture of how some people think spiritual growth in young teens should happen. This picture of spiritual growth could look something like this: Kid goes to camp...kid accepts Jesus...kid never looks back and grows closer to Jesus every day. I don't know about you, but I've never met a junior high student whose spiritual growth has been a perfectly straight line.

Scott *It's strange, though...when I first started doing junior high ministry, there was something in me that kind of thought it was going to look like this "straight line growth." Nobody really ever told me it would, but somehow I assumed it. Boy, was I wrong. And I'm betting I'm not the only one reading this who's made that assumption!*

Kurt Time to draw another line. In the second box, draw a line from the dot to the cross, but make sure it has some ups and downs in it...some "peaks and valleys." Make it look like one of those stock market graphs or the line on a hospital monitor that lets you know you're still alive. That's a more realistic picture, isn't it? There are good days and bad days, ups and downs, and peaks and valleys. In some ways, our spiritual growth is like the stock market: Despite inconsistencies, we grow over the course of time. While that may be an accurate picture for some, though, I don't think it truly portrays the spiritual growth of junior highers. We need a third picture.

In the third box, draw a line from the dot to the cross but make it as crazy as you want it to be—go all over the place. The only rule is that eventually it needs to end up making its way to the cross. Go ahead, have fun with it!

Now I want you to take a moment to look at all three boxes. The first two drawings may look cleaner, easier to explain, and safer—but they aren't an accurate picture of junior high spiritual growth. The third, however, is. Junior high spiritual growth is a crazy, topsy-turvy, two-steps-forward and three-steps-back, up-and-down, side-to-side journey! They're still getting closer to Jesus, but there's nothing clean, easy, or safe about it.

Scott

I remember when Kurt first showed these diagrams to me. I had an amazing sense of freedom *when I thought about it that way. Not that my desire to see a student move toward Jesus had changed at all—no way! But realizing that it not only* might *look messy sometimes, but that it was almost guaranteed to be messy…well, that helped me take a deep breath and not feel like such a failure on those "three-steps-back" days. I owe you for that perspective, KJ—thanks.*

Kurt

Let me give you a junior high ministry litmus test: How does the line in the third box make you feel? If it frustrates you, if you're tempted to straighten it out so it looks more like the first or second line, you probably shouldn't be involved in junior high ministry. I know that's a strong statement, but it's true.

Scott

OK, I know you're speaking strongly to make a point—and you make it well—but let's not go overboard, my friend. The third box frustrates me sometimes…and it frustrates some of the best junior high volunteers I know, too. But I don't think that means I should pull out of junior high ministry!

Because even though "steps backward" are to be expected in the life of a young teen, if it's a step away from Jesus, that bothers me. I just have to figure out what that student needs most when the line is doing a cartwheel. It's most likely not a rigid, line-straightening strategy, but it probably has something to do with love and acceptance…and another nudge in Jesus' direction. And if my blood pressure jacks up when I'm dealing with the messy line, well…that's OK sometimes! In fact, it might be a perfect opportunity to look in the mirror and reflect on my own path of following Jesus…and some of the twists and turns my own path has taken.

> What do I think?

What do I think?

Kurt

God hasn't called us to straighten the lines out but rather to journey alongside the students he's given us and gently point them to the cross...even though their lines are crooked.

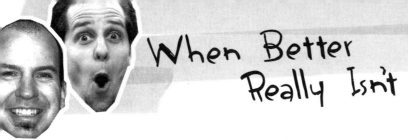

When Better Really Isn't

I bought my first cell phone about 10 years ago. It was a big, unwieldy brick that felt as though it weighed 5 pounds. I really couldn't carry it around with me because it wouldn't fit in my pocket, and trying to clip it on my belt proved disastrous on many levels. But the phone worked…it worked really well. It was so simple, so basic, and so easy to use.

Today I have a brand-new Treo Smartphone. This thing is the king of cell phones.

Well…the iPhone has come out since this was written…and I'm thinking it may be the new "king"—even though I don't have one yet. ⌒ But Kurt's illustration still works. ☺

In fact, the phone part of this thing is just a small part of its overall amazingness. It has a camera, a voice recorder, a full-sized keyboard, PowerPoint, Outlook, Word, and more. I can talk on the phone while I check my e-mails while I send a text message. I think I can even launch a missile!

The problem is, I really don't need all the bells and whistles…and I don't need to launch a missile.

Though I've actually considered needing a missile with a couple of parent phone calls I got this year…

I just want to talk on the phone once in a while. It seems as though all the attempts in recent years to simplify our lives have only served to make us busier. I can't have lunch with a friend without one of us being interrupted by a text message or dingy-ringy reminder about some upcoming appointment.

Sure, my new cell phone is a lot better than my first one…but maybe "better" isn't really.

I started in my first junior high ministry about 20 years ago. It was a big, unwieldy brick of a church. Our idea of technology was an overhead projector. Our idea of a creative event was renting out the roller rink. Most of the time we were combined with the high school ministry because space issues didn't allow us to separate. We had an old church bus that seemed to break down more often than it ran.

Today I lead what some people would consider the Treo of junior high ministries.

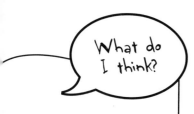

What do I think?

 Scott

Kurt, I've seen the plans for your new student center...your ministry is the iPhone-mulitplex-arena of junior high ministries...and yes, I am jealous.

Kurt

We've got just about everything a junior high ministry would want. In fact, our actual ministry to students is just a small part of our overall amazingness. We've got video cameras, jumbo screens, and expensive sound systems. We've got our own Chevy Suburban complete with a custom paint job. We have everything a junior high ministry needs and more.

The problem is, I really don't need all the bells and whistles. I just want to share life with junior high students. It seems like all the attempts in recent years to make our ministries bigger, cooler, and more exciting have only served to make them shallower. I can't sit down at my youth program to talk to a student without getting interrupted because something about the "program" needs my attention.

Sure, my new junior high ministry is a lot better than my first one...but maybe "better" isn't really.

 Scott

Well, maybe...and maybe not. See—I grew up in a church that sounds similar to the one you grew up in, Kurt...as far as the simple, non-techno, less-than-creative dimension goes. In fact, an overhead projector would have been cutting-edge for us (which perhaps explains why we didn't use one). But another thing we were missing was leaders with a burning desire to share life with junior high students. Actually, we often lacked any leaders at all. There just wasn't a vision in our church to really reach junior highers. And when there's a vision to reach students, I think it often starts with simply sharing life with them. But then as God begins to touch students' hearts and people start to dream of how more students could experience this life-changing power, often ministries move on to more imaginative, more resourceful ways to point students toward Jesus. Which I honestly think can be great! And I believe it's often the natural outflow of seeing students touched by this amazing love. Nothing wrong with that!

But some ministries seldom dream. Not about new ways to reach out to students…and often not about anything at all. The only dream is, "What are we going to do with those students next week?" Which hardly counts for a goal worthy of the God we serve and the students he loves!

The trick, as Kurt is pointing out, is that we need to make sure the ministry is serving the purpose it's designed for…instead of becoming a slave to the "bells and whistles"! The technology and program should always come way after building relationships with junior high students that translate into a relationship with God.

What do I think?

How to Become a Game-Running Guru

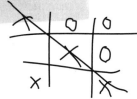

 Kurt When it comes to the current state of game playing in junior high ministries, here's what I know: I really like games, and I believe they're a fundamental part of a healthy ministry to young teenagers.

More and more youth workers are saying that games are overrated, that kids don't like games anymore, and that games are a big reason junior high ministry isn't taken seriously.

Those same youth workers still find themselves playing games in their junior high ministry from time to time, but they aren't very good at running them. As a result, the game time flounders, and youth workers point their fingers at the concept of games instead of at their prejudice toward games or their inability to run a game well.

 Scott Or *could it be that those youth workers are just putting more of their energy toward stimulating students to think? Isn't it possible that some youth workers, instead of thinking that games are overrated, are thinking that middle schoolers may have been underchallenged? So maybe they don't stink at running games, but they're really trying not to underestimate what can be done during youth group time. And as for me, I think that's kind of cool.*

Kurt If you've decided that your junior high ministry will never play another game, then you don't need to keep reading. You're free to continue prepping your 45-minute exegetical study of Leviticus that you plan to teach *seventh-graders*. For the rest of you, I'd like to share a few tips that will help make you a game-running guru!

Be energetic. If you're excited about a game, your kids will be, too. Your attitude can make or break the game.

Be organized. Be certain you know how to play the game before unleashing it on your students. Make sure you've brought the proper supplies. If it's a messy game, make sure you have stuff to protect the area and to clean up any mess. If the rules of the game call for 50 balloons, make 75.

Be clear. Simple, easy-to-understand games are the most effective. Avoid games that take 20 minutes to explain and only five minutes to play. When explaining the rules of a game, there are three guidelines: Keep them short, keep them simple, and keep everybody quiet until you're finished.

Be fair. Don't twist the score to let eighth-graders win. Don't invent rules halfway through the game. Don't give the seventh-grade girls a few "secret tips." Junior highers are notorious for yelling, "That's not fair!" When it involves a game, they're often right.

Be sensitive. Don't use games to purposely embarrass kids, and don't ridicule their performance. Don't force them to participate; they may have a good reason for declining.

I totally agree! One humiliating experience could push someone away from your ministry—but also away from God and his church. Being embarrassed is tough when you're an adult…and horrible when you're in junior high!

Be smart. Quit while you're ahead—always leave them wanting more. End each game on a high note. If a game is going poorly, quit before it turns disastrous! And don't play any game that you'd be uncomfortable playing in front of parents. If you think maybe you shouldn't play it…you shouldn't!

Be willing to mix it up. Not every middle schooler likes or is adept at every game. Strive for a balance between physical, mental, group, and individual games. And don't play kids' favorite games too often—they can become their least favorite if they play them every week.

Running games effectively isn't easy. But with a little practice, you can become a game-running guru!

This is fantastic advice on games! When a junior higher gets invited to do something—by his friend, his family, his church…whomever—I'm convinced that one of the first questions he's going to ask himself is, "Is it going to be fun?" And I don't think there's anything wrong with that! Am I going to be able to laugh a few times? Or am I going to have to stay straight-faced and serious?

Students may not say it this way, but they want to know if it's going to feel like a high-discipline classroom or a place of interactive relationship. When junior high students see me, the leader, laugh or play or engage in something really silly—I

> What do I think?

What do I think?

believe it breaks down some walls and shows students that I can see things from their angle. If you're thinking, *I'm really bad at the fun stuff,* think of an adult you know who's good at it, and get that person to help you! I bet you know someone *who fits that volunteer role!* Just don't underestimate what the fun factor can add to the environment of your ministry.

At the same time, I have one **huge caution.** If students mostly see a ministry as being about "fun stuff," they miss great chances to learn, grow, and move closer to Christ. Having a "the-best-games-and-activities-in-town" ministry can get some students to show up—for a while. But you and I both know that's not the reason we—or they—are involved! Our goal is to help students know and follow Jesus. Just don't underestimate your students' ability to engage in the more serious moments, too!

Predictions and Dreams

 Kurt

I've recently been asked two significant questions in two different forums. The first question: "What do you think youth ministry will look like in 50 years?" The second: "What are your dreams for junior high ministry?" Both are great questions…what do I *think* will happen and what do I *hope* will happen?

Fifty years is a long way off. Guessing (and that's exactly what it would be) what youth ministry will look like around the year 2058 sounds like a job for people way smarter than me.

But my dreams? I know what I dream for. So instead of making uncertain guesses, I'd like to spend a few moments sharing my dreams of the future in hopes that they may become reality…even if it takes 50 years.

 Scott

I'm like you on this one, Kurt—I love to dream about what it could be! In fact, one "theme" we had for all our volunteer junior high leaders is "Are You a Dreamer?"! Because I believe that's what you must be to see what God could have in store for junior high students! But as I read this, I honestly get a little fearful about what would happen if we don't dream God-sized dreams. And it kind of scares me. Pessimism isn't my normal approach—but junior high students could be way more vulnerable if more of us don't dream dreams similar to what you're suggesting, Kurt!

 Kurt

I dream of families that take more ownership when it comes to setting the spiritual temperature.

How would kids' lives be different if more moms and dads decided it wasn't the youth group's job to disciple their kids? How cool would it be if junior high youth workers had to cancel a few activities a year because parents demanded more time with their kids? What if more of our students saw their moms and dads living a life that was radically invaded by Jesus?

 Scott

I'd be elated if this could happen! But…these days I'm wondering if my junior high ministry sometimes gives off the wrong message here. "Don't worry, Mom and Dad, just drop off your kids, and we'll take care of them spiritually." How do I remind parents that they are the number one spiritual influence (positive…and negative) in their kids' lives? How do I encourage parents to play that role? We all know families have gigantic challenges already. If I don't find better ways to partner with parents…this dream turns into a nightmare.

We're still experimenting with the best ways to do this—learning as we go. We've sent e-mails and snail mail to parents with information on what we've been covering in our programs and "conversation starters" relating to what we're teaching in our programs.

We've also put on some events designed for junior highers and *their parents together*. Not every student comes, but when everybody has a parent along, it's less embarrassing. And parents have given us overwhelmingly positive feedback!

I dream of junior highers who believe in truth and know where it originates.

I may be old school, but I still believe in absolute truth that comes from the Word of God. I still believe that a biblical worldview is the most important item in a young teenager's survival kit.

"Old school" is "good school" in this case. But I wake up from this dream in a cold sweat when I worry about how well we're showing students how to use their Bibles, study their Bibles, learn from their Bibles. If we (and their parents) don't help young teens figure out how to engage with God's Word, will they become increasingly less familiar with the Bible? What if that happens? Am I showing them how to access the power?

When we teach, we have students bring their Bibles or use "loaner Bibles" at the church so they can look up the Scripture we use. Simple, but helpful! Student versions of the Bible can be really helpful, too. Also, explaining the tools that adults take for granted, like the concordance and topic index, can help students become familiar with their Bibles.

I dream of junior highers who are salt and light.

I dream of junior high students who rub shoulders with the world in such a way that truth gets put to the test and they find themselves wrestling with what they've been taught all their lives. After all, a truth wrestled through is a truth held on to. I dream that in these moments, junior highers will be able to confidently and compassionately model and share the good news of Jesus Christ.

Man, I can't fake pessimism on this one. I'm so hopeful! Junior highers are looking for hope and a better way to live, aren't they? When their friends who are following Jesus are really living differently…it's like a magnet to them. The junior highers I know don't seem to back down from the challenge to talk with their friends about real stuff. But am I challenging them often enough? Every week in our ministry we ask ourselves two questions: "What do we want students to know?" and "What do we want students to do?" If we can't answer those two things, the challenge won't be clear to students. And when students do follow through and respond to challenges, we love to tell those stories when we gather. It inspires other students and reminds them that it really is possible to live as salt and light! (And telling those stories stokes me back up all over again and encourages me to keep going!)

I dream of junior highers who are beginning to understand grace.

Not the "Jesus loves you and me and we're all OK" kind of grace. I'm talking about the big, wonderful, mysterious grace of our living God. I'm talking about the grace that makes any response other than surrendering to Christ impossible.

I dream of lots and lots of junior high youth workers.

OK, maybe now I really *am* dreaming! But I dream of a day when junior high ministry won't be the one ministry in the church that most volunteers avoid. I dream of a day when more churches are willing to invest more money into this amazing age group. I dream of a day when more people who are called to full-time ministry believe God is asking them to live out that calling by investing in the lives of young teens.

What will youth ministry look like in 50 years? I don't know! I don't even know what my junior high ministry will look like in 50 minutes. I'm hesitant to make guesses about the future. But I'm not afraid to dream!

I'm dreaming with ya, Kurt…and I know others are, too! Forgive me if it sounds grandiose…but I really believe that all of us doing junior high ministry today can catalyze the dreams of the future. Am I building up younger leaders and trying to help them catch the dream? Every year I like to play a little game with myself: Which eighth grader in my church is most likely to do junior high ministry some day? Ever asked yourself that question? Maybe students of that one eighth grader will be affecting the dream 50 years from now!

What do I think?

Uncool Is OK

 I was recently asked to speak at a gathering of youth workers. It wasn't until after I'd agreed that they told me the topic would be youth culture.

If I'd known before I agreed to speak that this was the topic, I would've certainly declined the invitation. I'm 40. I'm balding. I'm out of shape. My knees hurt. Frankly, I can't move fast enough to keep up with youth culture. I don't know if Jennifer Aniston and Vince Vaughn are getting married. I don't know the names of the children Brad and Angelina have adopted. I don't watch *Cribs, Made, Next,* or *Pimp My Ride*. I don't have piercings, tattoos, or those crazy ear plug things. I do, however, have a dorky "soul patch" under my lower lip that I grew about 10 years ago. Oh, and I have pretty sweet reading glasses.

Cool I am not.

So in front of a room of people hoping to learn about youth culture, I decided to publicly declare my uncoolness. I shared with them what I want to share with you: There are more important things in youth ministry than knowing the latest trends in youth culture. There are more important things than being able to quote funny movie lines and having a MySpace account. Maybe it's more important to:

Remember the little things. Young people often feel lost in the crowd. Remembering things such as a birthday, a prayer request they shared last week, a struggle they had at school, or a success story they shared is a big deal!

Practice the art of the second chance. And the third…and the fourth. As a youth worker, you're in a unique position to surprise teenagers with grace. Most of the time, you won't feel bound to enforce the rules the way parents, teachers, and other people in authority often do. Sure, there are times when rules must be enforced and consequences suffered, but look for opportunities to surprise middle schoolers with grace.

Put them first. Yeah, middle school students like games, music, videos, and all the stuff that goes into a typical youth night. But more than that, they like it when a caring adult puts all that stuff on hold to look them in the eye.

Stick around for awhile. So much about a middle schooler's world is spinning and changing! Being a source of security in an unstable time may be one of the most important things you can offer.

One way we try to tackle this issue is by encouraging our small group leaders to take a group of students all the way through junior high—to commit to a three-year run with their sixth graders. Sounds daunting at first…and we don't make that challenge the first week. But most of our leaders end up doing it—to the benefit of their students!

 Sure, watch MTV every once in awhile. Swap out your issue of Newsweek for an issue of Rolling Stone or Vibe. Turn off the Fox News Channel and turn on VH1 for an hour. A basic understanding of youth culture is important. But maybe there's more important stuff.

 Man—I completely agree with you, Kurt…you're not cool at all! ☺

As I was reading your words and nodding my head (I didn't want to interrupt too much), I thought about my first years in junior high ministry. "Am I cool enough?" was actually one of the questions I was asking myself when I jumped into it. I was past 30 when I started junior high ministry, and the "cool" question was right at the front of my mind. It didn't take me long to realize that it was the wrong question to be asking. Junior highers weren't most concerned about that.

The suggestions in this section seem right on track with what they are concerned with. I think it was Wayne Rice who said, "Adolescents will gravitate toward the oldest person who will take them seriously." You can "be cool" and miss that chance to take a student seriously. But if you lean into Kurt's suggestions, they'll feel valued and cared for…and probably more open to God's work in their lives!

P.S.—As of this writing, Jennifer Aniston and Vince Vaughn are not together. But since that doesn't really matter for this topic, feel free to turn the page.

What do I think?

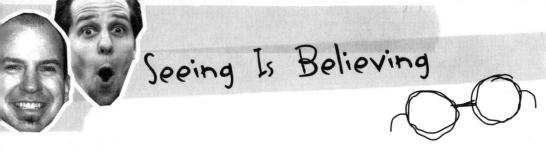

Seeing Is Believing

Kurt Seeing is believing—what young people see when they look at your ministry is what they'll believe about it. This is especially true of kids visiting youth group for the first time. They don't know you, the other leaders, or most of the teenagers involved. All they know is what they see.

What do junior highers see when they look at your youth group?

As a case study, I've listed several things first-timers see in my ministry at Saddleback—the good, the bad, and the ugly. I'll let you wrestle through what they might believe about our ministry as a result. When you get a chance, I'd suggest you take a few minutes to do the same with your own ministry setting.

The entrance to our meeting space—A first-time guest will see a big banner with our logo hanging on the side of our tent (first, they'll see that we meet in a goofy tent). They'll also see a cool-looking Suburban with our ministry name painted on it. As they get closer, they'll notice an entrance blocked by all the "cool" kids standing around and talking to each other. If they have the guts to approach, they probably won't be greeted—if they are, it'll be by an overly aggressive student leader.

Scott *Vulnerability—I love it. Kurt and I have actually been able to stand in the back of each other's ministry space and just watch. And I did get "approached" by one of his hard-hitting leaders. But I think he's being pretty tough on himself here. This article kind of highlights (read: exaggerates) the negatives; part of me wants to defend him: You're not so bad, Kurt! But it's so easy for us to defend our ministries. Is it easy to be brutally honest about them? Is it possible that brutal honesty in our weakest areas might be exactly what we need in order to improve them? I think it's downright genius to take a few minutes—while your ministry is going on—to put on "first-timer glasses" and imagine how you'd feel if you didn't know anybody.*

Kurt **Our atmosphere**—Once inside, they'll see Xboxes, video screens, Ping-Pong tables, and bulletin boards covered in pictures. They'll also see that one group of guys dominates the video game area, rarely giving up their seats. They'll notice large groups of kids clustered in circles that seem almost impenetrable. And they'll see loners sitting by themselves.

I've heard it said that the feel of your ministry might be the most important dimension of it. What a student "senses" actually speaks way louder than any lesson that's taught, any song that's sung, any words that get spoken. It's the hidden curriculum…and it can draw someone in or push someone away. As leaders, how do we manage this intangible aspect, giving students the vision for their role? We've tried using student "tour guides" for a time—I think we might be on to something, but we haven't hit the bull's-eye on this one yet.

 Our adult leaders—They'll see a few adults hanging out with teenagers, but upon closer inspection they'll notice that most of the adults are either huddled together or "policing" the room like chaperones.

 There are good and bad aspects of that. If your adult leaders like to huddle together, it probably means they enjoy being with each other, which helps them be effective! Just help them understand that this is a time to focus on students. Then create a different time for them to hang out with each other.

I could go on and on, but you get the point. It's important to look at every aspect of our ministry on a regular basis through the eyes of new kids. Sometimes, if we're honest with ourselves, it hurts. It's tough for me to highlight these three areas as I write this.

Our ministry will never be perfect, and I expect yours won't be, either. Let's agree together to work toward leading junior high ministries that help young people "see" that they matter to us and to God.

What do I think?

Encouraging Parents

 Kurt

A few weeks ago, I went to the local Starbucks for an early-morning writing session, and something unusual caught my attention.

I was the only person there for the first few minutes, but as I was digging my laptop out of its bag and setting up my mobile office, a middle-aged dad and his junior high–aged daughter came in, ordered a couple of drinks, and sat down at a table in the corner. For the next hour they talked, laughed, read the Bible, and prayed together. The fact that he was spending one-on-one time with his daughter, and that she seemed to be enjoying herself, got me thinking…

Dads are important—especially to young girls. As I observed the interaction between dad and daughter, I was reminded of how vital a role dads play in the lives of their daughters. Sure it's important for moms to take their girls out for coffee, but girls also long for and need a healthy relationship with their dads.

 Scott

Dads are super-important to young girls! But I think they're especially super-important to sons, at least as much as they are to daughters! Honestly, it might (or might not) be a shade easier to have a conversation with a junior high daughter; conversation seems to flow more readily from some young girls' mouths. Still, the young guy is taking cues as to what it means to be a man…and where's the first place he'll look? His dad!

 Kurt

Junior high kids like quality time with their parents. They may not ask for it, and they may not seem very excited when the idea is suggested, but junior high kids like spending time with Mom and Dad.

The key to good quality time? Timing! My hunch is that the girl in Starbucks is a morning person. It's a natural time for her dad to target as quality time.

Scott

One more thought on the gender angle…a young girl might get amped up about sitting at a table in a coffee shop across from Dad. But try that with lots of sons, and you may not get nearly the quantity of word-exchange as with a girl! Often, guys are better at interactions when there's something else going on—passing a football to each other, riding bikes, or sitting on snowmobiles. I know a dad who learned snowboarding as a middle-aged guy, just so he could do something that his son loved with him!

Awkward moments are going to happen, and that's OK. As I watched their time together unfold, I noticed several moments of awkward silence when it was obvious neither the daughter nor the dad knew where to take the conversation. They'd sit quietly for a few moments, and then one of them would push the conversation forward.

 Being OK with awkward is easier said than done. But it's huge. And awkward is guaranteed to happen. Some parents think that if there are uncomfortable moments, they're doing something wrong. But they're not! Remember…much of middle school is bathed in awkwardness!

 Quality time is risky, but rewarding. Junior high kids are going to roll their eyes the first time a parent invites them to share a little one-on-one time, and the awkward moments can frazzle any parent. But the rewards far outweigh the risk.

Even parents who are good at this need encouragement. The next day I headed back to Starbucks and, much to my surprise, the father/daughter combo had beaten me there! An hour later, as they got up to leave, I decided to pull the dad aside to encourage him. I told him that I'm the dad of a junior high girl, too, and that seeing him spending quality time with his daughter encouraged me to do more of the same. His eyes watered up a little, and with a crack in his voice, he thanked me. "I know it's important, and I'm trying to do it more often," he said. "Thanks for the encouragement."

How can youth ministers do a better job ministering to parents? One of the best ways is to simply encourage them in their journey. Maybe the story of the Starbucks dad is worth sharing with your kids' parents. Maybe the next time you catch them doing something great, you can tell them so.

What do I think?

Why?

 Kurt If you've worked with junior high or middle school students for any period of time, you've certainly been asked, "Why?"

 Scott *Sorry to interrupt after only one sentence, but not only might other people ask you "Why?" sometimes you probably ask yourself that very question! Aren't there easier ministry areas? or Am I really making much impact? But having a rock-solid answer to this question really helps on those days when your junior high girls are more into giddiness than godliness or your junior high boys focus more on farting than what they're feeling.*

 Kurt I get these questions all the time: "Why did you start working with junior high-ers?" "Why have you stuck with it?" "Why do you plan to continue?" Your reasons may differ, but here are five of the biggest reasons I choose young teenagers as my ministry focus.

It's my calling. I can't tell you the exact moment I felt called to this ministry. The skies didn't part, and God's voice didn't wake me in the middle of the night. I simply feel called to this age group. My friends and ministry colleagues don't understand it, and sometimes I question it myself, but I'm convinced that God has wired me and called me to dedicate my life to this wonderful, hard-to-figure-out, frustrating, thankless, joy-filled thing called junior high ministry. If I sense God is calling me elsewhere, I'll be obedient, but until then I'm staying put.

 Scott *This is an area where I'm different than you, Kurt. I was happy doing ministry with adults almost a decade ago when I got challenged to look into serving students. I still get skittish about calling it my "calling," but I can tell you that I'm loving it, and I sense God using me in it. And I've got no doubt that's where God wants me right now. So maybe that's what we mean by calling…so I won't worry about it!*

 Kurt **It's fun.** I'm 40 years old, so lock-ins aren't as fun as they used to be. I don't find a whole lot of joy in sneaking out at midnight with a bunch of seventh-grade guys to toilet-paper a house.

But pound for pound, it's impossible for me to think of a ministry that's more fun than this! Summer camps, mission trips, small groups, dodge ball, skits, ministry teams, relay races—these are just a few of the highlights. Sure there's a lot of work involved, but working at having fun isn't a bad gig!

And I've got friends who wear a suit and tie to work every single day…which I don't mind missing out on.

 It's overlooked. I have a soft spot for the underdog.

Junior high ministry is definitely the underdog of the local church setting. I fight for my share of the budget, for the use of facilities, and for announcement space in the bulletin. Sure, every ministry area fights for the same things, but somehow we always have to fight just a little bit harder. Young teenagers need advocates. They need adults who believe in their cause and are willing to fight on their behalf.

 This seems true everywhere I go! The women's ministry or the men's breakfast can petition the board for resources, but I haven't seen many groups of junior highers making presentations at those board meetings. They also need someone to believe in them. I'm honestly still disappointed that so many adults look down their noses in judgment at "kids these days." Have they forgotten what it's like to be 13? Well, probably. That's OK. We just need to help them remember by waving the banner…and by telling the positive stories about how students are making a difference today!

 It's important. We don't need the latest surveys or statistics to show us that the world is different today than it was five or 10 years ago. Kids are growing up faster but are less equipped to deal with those life changes. They're both saturated by, and vulnerable to, culture. More and more of their parents are divorcing. They live in a post-9/11 world that has chipped away at their sense of security. If junior high ministry was important when we were their age, it's even more so today.

It's working! Junior high ministry works. It's a pretty simple formula, really: Caring Adult + Junior High Student = Good Stuff! Sure, we like to complicate it with an emphasis on creativity, programs, snazzy youth rooms, training seminars, and columns in magazines from people who seem to have it all together, but the simple truth is that junior high ministry works. Caring adults all across

What do I think?

What do I think?

the globe are spending time with goofy, insecure, rude, obnoxious young teenagers…and it's working!

Why do we do it? Because it works.

Scott

Here's a challenge that can re-stoke your commitment to students: Why not take 90 seconds right now and do this same exercise that Kurt just did? Make a list of four or five statements that describe "Why I'm working with junior highers."

I bet you'll energize yourself, even if it's been a challenging season! We'll get you started: I work with junior highers because it's…

Do Your Lessons T.E.A.C.H.?

 Kurt I'm guessing that if you're reading this, you most likely minister to junior high students in a local church context.

If this is true, I'm also fairly certain that you're expected to engage your students in some sort of formal Christian education. How that looks for you, I don't know.

In my setting, our formal teaching takes place in three arenas: the large group setting, the small group setting, and individually. We have a weekly large group program that runs simultaneously with our adult worship service. In this 60-minute program, we dedicate 20 minutes for fun programming, 20 minutes for music, and 20 minutes for a formal teaching time. In our small groups we set aside about 45 minutes of the evening for deep study, discussion, and prayer. For our individual students, we've written a variety of self-paced workbooks, Bible studies, and journals.

Over the years I've taught a lot of lessons: large group "sermons," small group discussions, object lessons, case studies, on-the-go active learning, and so on. You name it, I've done it!

It pains me to admit this, but on "rare" occasions (say, three times a month!), my lessons miss the mark. I'm sharper than most, so I've learned to spot the very subtle signs: students snoring in the front row, paper airplanes flying through the room, glazed-over eyes staring into space as drool slowly drips from the mouth. I think it's a privilege to present the good news of Jesus Christ to students, and I often find myself frustrated that I haven't been able to do so in a way that holds my students' attention.

Scott *"Sidebar thought"…which of these two is tougher to do: keep the attention of students or keep the attention of adults? Before you answer too quickly, think for a minute about another question. Which group gives you more clues as to whether you're really holding their attention? Hmm. If you're talking to a group of adults and they're bored stiff or not following what you're saying, what do they do? They maintain eye contact, nod their heads every once in a while, and appear to be very interested. Try the same thing with a group of students, and what do they do? I've found that they'll give a wet willy to the guy next to them, turn around and start a conversation with the girl in the row behind them…or any of the other subtle signs Kurt mentions above! Lots of people would prefer to teach a group of adults—maybe because the feedback isn't so immediate and honest…sometimes painfully!*

Kurt While there's certainly no magic formula for teaching success, here's a filter that's helped me: I evaluate each lesson by looking at what I've prepared and asking myself, *Does this lesson T.E.A.C.H.?*

Is it True? Is it biblically sound? Are verses used in context? Is the whole of Scripture considered? When putting a lesson together, it's easy to proof-text (take verses out of context to prove our point). I've fallen into the trap many times of starting with my version of truth or my "soapbox" of the moment and then searching the Scriptures for a verse that seems to back it up.

Scott *I completely agree! I often tell students in our ministry that it's a good thing we're counting on God's truth...and not just "Scott's best ideas for surviving junior high." When I realized this for the first time, it actually took some pressure off me. I still had to do the hard work of figuring out how to take biblical counsel and help junior highers understand and apply it...but the source was wisdom so much greater than mine! John 7:16 is a verse that has anchored my thinking on this, when Jesus said, "My teaching is not my own. It comes from him who sent me."*

Kurt **Is it Encouraging?** Does this lesson motivate and encourage students toward some sort of action or commitment? If I'm teaching a hard truth, am I doing so in an encouraging way? Remember, it's the good news!

Scott *I mostly get what you're saying...and think that almost all lessons should be encouraging. But are there exceptions? Like what if sometimes a lesson should be more of a "warning" or what-could-happen-if-God's-Word-is-ignored? We just talked about suicide last weekend, and while part of the interview we did was "encouraging"—I'm not sure that's the word I'd use to describe it best. Then again, we really need an "E" word to make the acrostic work.*

Kurt **Is it Applicable?** Does this study or lesson apply to the world of a junior higher? Have I made the effort to make the biblical truth actually true to them? Does this lesson equip them to live out their faith beyond the walls of the church?

Scott *Right on. For every lesson we try to ask, "What do I want them to know, and what do I want them to do?"*

Kurt **Is it Clear?** Is this lesson easily understood? Is the main point clear? Is it logical? Does it make sense? Does it have a "flow"?

Scott *Here's a great test...can you state the point of the lesson in **one sentence?** If you can't...there's a good chance it's not clear! When they get in the car afterwards and*

Mom or Dad asks, "What did you talk about?" they should be able to say it in a sentence (not that they will...but I try to make sure they could...)!

Is it Humorous? *You don't have to be drop-dead funny, but junior highers like to laugh, and they like to have fun. They expect Bible studies to be boring...surprise them by adding a few humorous stories and some fun interaction. When students are smiling and laughing with each other during your lesson, they're also learning more.*

This is what I've learned: Just because I'm talking, I'm not necessarily teaching; and just because I'm teaching, students aren't necessarily learning. Running my lessons through the T.E.A.C.H. filter seems to have helped. Eyes still glaze over occasionally, but there's much less drool.

What do I think?

What Makes a Good Junior High Worker?

 John Allen is a fantastic volunteer on my junior high team at Saddleback. Every weekend, John sits smack-dab in the center of our crowd of students during our program. This summer John went to camp as a counselor and spent a week in a cabin filled with seventh-grade guys. John is 75 years old!

You probably aren't. You're probably much younger, much cooler, much more athletic, and much better at throwing a dodge ball than John. (He would, however, be a great dodge-ball target…not too quick on his feet!) Here are just a few things, though, that I've learned about junior high ministry from John.

Good junior high workers live a balanced life. John loves our ministry, but he loves other stuff, too. He's got other hobbies, other friends, and a girlfriend whom he enjoys spending time with. It would be easy for him to give our ministry a bigger chunk of his time, but he's decided not to. For John, the best way to continue to enjoy junior high ministry is to be sure he still enjoys a lot of other things.

 Can I push this to the next level? If you have a volunteer in your ministry and you start to see that his or her life is starting to get a little "junior-high-centric," you might have a problem. Over the years, I've run into an occasional case where a volunteer doesn't seem to have any friends or interests outside of the students in his or her group. And each time I've seen it, it's been a warning sign of an unhealthy lifestyle.

 Good junior high workers know themselves. Earlier I joked that John would make a great dodge-ball target. He would if he were dumb enough to allow himself to play. John understands his strengths, his weaknesses, and his life-stage. When he went to camp with us, he requested a co-counselor because he likes to take an afternoon nap. On the weekends, he sometimes slips out when the music is too loud. John knows where he adds the most value to our team, and he focuses on those areas.

Good junior high workers are comfortable in their own skin. Granted, John's skin is a bit wrinkly, but he wears it well. He enjoys his role as the ministry grandpa. He doesn't try to act like he's 14 years old—he doesn't even try to act like he's 24, 34, 44, 54, or 64 years old! He is who he is, and he likes it. It should come as no surprise that students, who live in a culture of pretense, see John as a breath of fresh air and are drawn to him.

Scott *Sounds like John also knows that junior highers need a "caring adult" way more than they need "another friend." I think that's a big misunderstanding sometimes…wanting students to see us as their friend. There aren't enough adults who really listen, really care, really take them seriously. And that's worth way more than merely trying to act like a young teen along with them to gain their acceptance!*

Kurt Good junior high workers actually like young teens. Before joining our volunteer team, John taught eighth grade for 35 years. Upon his retirement he began to pray about getting more involved in ministry. He says he just couldn't shake his call to junior high students and felt our ministry was the place he was being led to serve. John not only understands junior highers and recognizes the importance of ministry to this age group…he actually likes junior high students. He enjoys their rowdiness, their quirks, and their brutal honesty.

Scott *What's hidden between the lines here is that there's no one "model" junior high worker! As I think through the best leaders in our ministry, there are some strong, young, good-looking 20-somethings, but I also know these solid leaders: a 40-something out-of-shape truck driver, a middle-aged-sharp-thinking CEO, a couple of young moms, a young married couple…and an almost 70-year-old leader named Paul, who could still probably knock out Kurt's friend John with a dodge ball. No offense intended.*

Kurt Good junior high workers lead "up." John isn't the point person of our ministry, and you may not be, either. However, John is constantly looking for ways to lead from the middle of the pack, to be a leader among leaders. For example, we're thinking of creating a pictorial directory for each of our four weekend programs. This way, the volunteers who work during each hour would have a booklet full of the names and faces of students who regularly attend that service. It's a big undertaking and one that I hope we're able to pull off. It wasn't my idea, though. It was John's. He noticed that in large settings

What do I think?

What do I think?

it's simply too difficult to remember names the way we should, and he suggested we do something about it instead of just accepting the status quo.

 Another hidden lesson I'm picking up here…sounds like you really listen to your volunteers, Kurt. It's easy for those of us who are the point person of our ministries to fall into the trap of thinking, I'm the pro here, I'll decide what stuff we do, and the rest of the team is just here to help pull off my great ideas. I've fallen into that trap more than once. I'll bet right now on our junior high leadership teams there are people with some super innovations for our ministries, and they just need an invitation to talk about it! Matter of fact, just this weekend I wrote down the name of one of our volunteers whom I need to call; she's a realtor with some great ideas of how we can invite more leaders into our ministry!

Kurt John doesn't know what an iPod is. He didn't see any of the big summer movies. He doesn't wear Dickies shorts and Vans. He's easily tired, often sore, and likely to go home a bit early. He's also one of the best junior high workers I've ever known.

Scott *Dickies shorts? Are you serious?*

Leadership Made Easy

 Kurt Well, OK…the title of this section is a little deceptive—there's really nothing easy about leadership. If being a leader were easy, then everybody would do it. The truth is that most people are followers. Because you bought this book, though, I'm betting you're in some sort of leadership role. And because you're reading this particular section, I'm betting your leadership role is likely in a junior high ministry setting (move over, Sherlock!).

 Scott *Most people are followers? Maybe. But I also think you can make a case that most people are leaders at least somewhere in their lives! Maybe it's at home, or at work, or with a few friends, or a younger sibling…but I think most of us have a chance (and maybe even a responsibility) to lead somewhere in our lives. And I think this section has valuable thoughts for leaders and "nonleaders" alike.*

 Kurt If we were to ask 100 people what makes a good junior high leader, we'd probably get 100 different answers. Personally, I believe there are leadership qualities that transcend context. In other words, a lot of the leadership qualities needed to be a good CEO are the same as those needed to be a good president, which are the same as those needed to be a good junior high worker. These qualities are numerous, but let me give you three that I try to remind myself of every day.

Be Ethical—Integrity, honesty…however you define what it means to be ethical, recent history is scattered with far too many examples of corporate, political, and religious leaders who fell short in this area. Each day, you're faced with lots of opportunities to lead ethically. Here are a few examples of what ethical leadership might look like in junior high ministry:

- Not playing favorites with the "cool" or "church" kids
- Keeping good financial records of the money spent in your ministry
- If you get paid, making the most of the time you're "on the clock"
- Not exaggerating the stories you tell in your lessons
- Saying an honest "no" to a request instead of saying "yes" and becoming bitter

 Scott *Most people probably read that last section and say, "Yep, hard to argue with that stuff." And I agree! But it seems like most often people slowly slide into ethical problems rather than jump into them. I know of a junior high leader who ended up getting fired from a church for ripping off the youth ministry budget. But it started with charging "just a few" personal expenses to his ministry and justifying it because his salary was*

so low. One thing led to another—and by the time it was over he'd robbed the church of thousands of dollars. Is there anywhere where you're slipping—even just a little tiny bit—when it comes to the ethical stuff?

Be Effective—A good definition of effectiveness is "doing the right things." In life and ministry, there are lots of good opportunities, but effective leaders recognize that not every good opportunity is a good opportunity for them. Just because someone has an idea for an activity or suggests a new curriculum or finds a great new service project doesn't mean you need to add it to your junior high calendar!

My phone rings several times a week with opportunities for our ministry that "are just too good to pass up"—the door-to-door fundraiser selling lifetime supplies of cellophane, the traveling evangelist who uses a yo-yo and a watermelon in his presentation, and so on. I almost always pass them up.

When you're done reading this, I encourage you to think about your junior high ministry and make a list of the things that are most important to its effectiveness. Be sure not to let other stuff crowd these items out.

Man, this is a difficult one for me! Maybe partially because I love new ideas, and my "Stuff to Try" list is always a mile long. But that can really take me off track if I let it. I have to be disciplined (I hate that word) to focus on what I know will serve students best, and to have my ear continually open to God for his guidance on this one. P.S.—Kurt, you told me that yo-yo watermelon guy was a real success in your group. You weren't exaggerating, were you? That wouldn't be ethical.

Be Efficient—A good definition of efficiency is "doing things right." Junior high ministry is notorious for being run inefficiently. We're messy. We get home from trips late. We forget to make a flier. When we do make a flier, it's full of typos. We have a hard time staying within our budget. We procrastinate. Sound familiar? Being efficient takes work, but it's incredibly rewarding for you as a leader and for the ministry you're leading.

When I was growing up, I would constantly find shortcuts when doing chores such as mowing the lawn or washing the car. My dad would find mistakes in my work and say, "Kurt, it's funny that you never seem to have time to do it right the first time, but you always have time to do it over again." Efficiency is the art of learning how to do it right the first time.

OK, Kurt, you said I could speak freely, so I will. I think you're being too gentle here. Some of us aren't just "inefficient"; we're downright lazy. And it shouldn't be so! Feel free to think I'm exaggerating if you want to, but sometimes in youth ministry we "let ourselves get away with stuff" because no one's watching closely…and it's easier. God's

not honored by that, and neither is your church. Some of you reading this might be in no danger of this, but I'm convinced that some of us are. What we're doing is way too important to give less than our best. Let's do it right—together!

Kurt Being a leader isn't easy, but because you are one, you might consider helping your cause by being one who's ethical, effective, and efficient.

What do I think?

Living the Good Life

 Kurt My friend Brett Janzen lived the good life. That is until his sudden death a few weeks ago at age 42. Brett had been a youth pastor his entire adult life and spent the past 11 years ministering at a great church in a fantastic coastal community in southern California. Sounds pretty good, doesn't it? It gets better.

Brett was a good husband. He was married to his wife, Lynette, for over 20 years. I'm pretty sure all my friends love their wives, but there was something different about Brett's love. I wish I could explain it, but I can't. The depth of his love for Lynette has been made evident by the deep loss that her eyes try, but fail, to hide.

Brett was a good dad. He wasn't out five nights a week, even though youth ministry makes this far too easy. Brett wasn't traveling the nation on the youth pastor speaking tour, even though he was more qualified than most who do. Brett was too busy for that stuff…too busy being Brooke's dad.

Brett was a good friend. His memorial was one of the biggest I've ever attended. The auditorium was packed with more than 1,000 people. Certainly a lot were family and youth group members, but the vast majority were people who considered him a friend. His circle of friends was massive, extending well beyond his comfortable little Christian bubble and out into the community he served. He was a good friend to many and a great friend to a lucky few.

Brett was a good servant. Maybe even too good. I can't count the times I asked him, "Brett, can't you find somebody else to do this…have you ever thought about delegating?" But that just wasn't Brett's style. He lived the motto that so many other leaders simply say for effect: "Don't ask anybody to do something you're not willing to do yourself." I believe Brett's servant-leadership is what set him apart from so many leaders, and it may well be what's earned him the highest of rewards he's now enjoying.

Brett was a good time. He was rarely without a smile. I always felt better about myself after spending time with him.

He understood the value of fun and made sure he left time in his life to do the things he loved. He surfed several times a week and spent his last hours racing motocross. In John 10:10, Christ says that he came to give life to the fullest. Brett took him up on that promise.

I hope ministry is good for you right now; it is for me. I hope you've had some good events. I hope you've shared a few good lessons. I hope you've had some good conversations with students. Heck, I even hope you've had pretty good attendance! I'm hoping for all those things. But today, when I'm done writing this, I'm going to pray that everyone reading it will make a new commitment to what matters most…living the good life.

 Wow.

Maybe reading this made you think the same thing I did: I wish I could have known Brett.

He sure sounds like an amazing guy.

There's another thing it makes me think of, too. If my life were to end this month, how would people remember me? Do you think about that very often? I actually do. And sometimes I feel great about what they might remember. But other times, well…let's just say it puts things in perspective for me. What about you? What kind of friend would those close to you say you were? Would your spouse say that you treasured him or her as a gift God's given to you? Would your kids remember the time you spent with them—even when you could have been doing something that "appeared" more productive? If you have the guts, do a little inventory of how you've been handling the things in life that matter most. Be ruthlessly honest. Celebrate the places you're doing well! And make a decision to do something specific to change the areas you know need changing. Let's all take a cue from Brett and live the good life. It's within reach.

What do I think?

16 Ways to Tell If You're a Junior High Youth Worker

 You might be a junior high youth worker if...

...you've thought about growing your hair and shaving your goatee but just can't. Personally, I also insist on wearing baggy shorts, Vans shoes, and surf shirts. Look, if I wanted to wear Dockers and a button-down, I'd work for Microsoft...or be a high school pastor.

...you've rented *The Princess Bride* to show at a lock-in. This movie's a great reminder that we don't have to be edgy or controversial to have fun. If we aren't waving the banner of good, clean fun for our students, who is?

...your spouse works part time at Starbucks and still brings home a bigger paycheck. Let me remind you of something you've certainly told yourself before: You didn't get into this for the money. Besides, free iced mochas are a pretty good perk!

...you've toilet-papered your senior pastor's house. It didn't sound like a great idea at first, but once you got there it felt pretty good, huh?

...you've been blamed for a stain on the carpet in the fellowship hall. Chances are it was the junior high ministry, but did the church janitor ever think to question those fruit-punch-loving senior adults?

...you used to play Chubby Bunny. Did a student really choke to death playing this game? I'm not sure, but I'm done playing. Additionally, I've sold all my marshmallow stock due to plummeting sales.

...you've given away a WWJD bracelet as a prize. It was probably a few years ago, and you've likely tried to block it from your memory. Remember...the road to recovery begins with recognition.

...you've used a VeggieTales clip as a teaching tool. I can't explain it, but this is still a guaranteed winner. My favorite clip of all time: the little soldier peas mocking Joshua in *Josh and the Big Wall!*

...you've considered creating your own blog. I don't really know for sure what a blog is, but I've thought about creating one.

...you've spent hard-earned vacation time in a cabin full of seventh-graders. You didn't sleep much and went back to work in worse shape than when you left, but lives were changed, and you'd do it again next week if you were asked.

...you've thought about quitting—today! I'm not sure if a day goes by that I don't think about transitioning to an easier ministry area. I'm not sure if a day goes by that God doesn't remind me of the importance of my calling.

...you've been the victim of students pouring warm water into your hand while you slept. Like I said, not a day goes by...

...you really want an iPod. OK, you don't have to be a junior high worker to really want an iPod. But you do have to be a junior high worker to figure out how to convince the church elders that the junior high department really needs an iPod!

...you've bought a Palm Pilot but never use it. You will, however, use your iPod. Trust me.

...you've caught yourself telling a booger joke in your adult small group. Or you've giggled because you "cut one," and nobody knew it was you.

...you've had high school students return to say thanks. They hardly ever say it when they're in junior high, but they will eventually.

 ...if you think any of these are good enough to add (I didn't feel like I should interrupt the flow of what's above)...

...you've Googled song lyrics for music you'd never listen to on your own. *But you didn't want to admit to students you had no idea what the band was singing...and you also care about what's hitting their eardrums.*

...you wish you had a dime for every time you've heard someone say, "You must be really special to work with the junior highers. I could never do that."

...you've been hit in the head by a dodge ball or other game-oriented projectile...and for a split second you got really ticked! *Then you remembered how your example speaks louder than your teaching—or maybe you remembered a while later.*

What do I think?

...you've sat in a small group conversation and wondered to yourself, *Are we making any progress here at all?* There's blitzing chatter about movies, friends, crushes, miscellaneous silliness...and you're so far down the rabbit trail you're not sure how you can pull it back.

...you've gotten a rare e-mail from a parent, saying, "You have no idea how much you mean to my son." I can live off one of those encouragements for weeks...and sometimes I have to.

It's an odd group we're part of—being a junior high worker—and sometimes you feel like you have to be a member in order to "get it." But when I think about what God does with my meager efforts, I'd pledge all over again—wouldn't you?

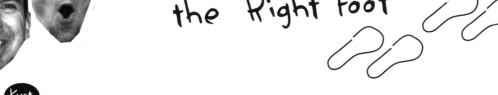

Kurt I'm 38, and there's not much I like about it—but I can scrape together two positives. First, I've finally realized I'm just not cool anymore, so I've quit trying. I've shaved my sideburns and openly admit I listen to talk radio. Second, I get to spend a lot more time encouraging younger junior high ministers.

A lot of the 20-something junior high ministers I hang out with ask me the same question: "How do I start out right so I can last?" That's a great question, and it gives me hope that, in time, there will be a lot more 38-year-old junior high workers. Here's my top five list of how to start out on the right foot.

Scott *I can't resist busting in early...even before you give your list, KJ. Just the fact that someone's humble enough to ask an "old-timer" like Kurt for tips on how to go the distance is a great sign. I love getting tips from people who're further down the road than I am—and it's really helped!*

Kurt **1. It all starts with your best tool...you.** Before you focus on Friday night outreach events, fun camp games, and attention-grabbing lesson illustrations, focus on yourself. You don't get a healthy junior high ministry without a healthy leader. Cultivate your relationship with God, protect your time with him, and pray David's prayer every day: "Search me, O God, and know my heart; test me and know my anxious thoughts. See if there is any offensive way in me, and lead me in the way everlasting" (Psalm 139:23-24).

Scott *This one sounds "obvious"...but I think it's exactly the right place to start. I have to remind myself of this over and over again. I'm actually God's child first...and his soldier second. When I'm really connected to the reality that God's crazy about me, independent of my "ministry output," I'm actually more effective in ministry! When was the last time you had a conversation with God about how your heart's doing?*

2. To start out on the right foot, keep your left foot out of your mouth. If you're just starting out in a ministry position, it's likely someone was doing the job before you showed up. Be wise about what you say right out of the gate. In a sad effort to gain your trust, some kids, parents, and volunteers will speak poorly of the previous leader. Don't do the same. And don't make grand promises you may later need to take back. In your first few months, the wisest thing you can do is listen and watch a lot more than you talk.

In addition, I'd say this: Ask a whole bunch of questions when you're in a new ministry position. Sit down and make a list of all the stuff you're wondering about. Then think about which questions should be asked of parents, of kids, of volunteers…maybe even of the senior pastor. Keep in mind that everyone's opinions will be just that: their opinions. But learning their perspective will really help you decide what your next move should be.

3. Don't make hasty changes. As you listen and watch, you'll soon identify areas that need change, even if you're stepping into a successful, established ministry. Because you bring fresh eyes to the ministry, you'll notice lots of things that those who've been around a while have gotten used to or have overlooked. It's tempting to come in and clean house. Resist this temptation—decide you're going to be patient and slow as you make changes.

Agreed. I wanted to make a few changes the minute I walked into my current position! But doing that too early can send the message, "You knuckleheads have been doing it all wrong!"

4. Check your pride at the door. If you didn't know already, you soon will: It's not about you! It's not your show, it's God's. If you got into ministry to somehow boost your own sense of worth, get out now. Far too many ministries have been ruined by prideful, insecure leaders who refuse to share the load. You're not the hero—you're a servant-leader who empowers others to use their gifts to make a difference.

So you're saying that renaming the winter retreat after myself was a bad idea?

5. Gain trust. Here are a few people whose trust you need to gain: parents, students, parents, senior pastor, parents, your supervisor, and parents. Gaining trust takes time, but you can do it! The best way to start gaining trust is by paying attention to the four previous *tips*.

By the way, I thought of a couple more things I like about being 38. I'm not yet 40. And God is still calling me to minister to junior highers!

So you're over 41 now—and older *than I am—but are you going to mention that?*

What do I think?

A Different Kind of Superhero

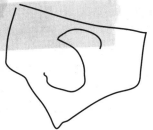

 Kurt Superheroes are in vogue right now. I recently read an article that labeled superhero movies, such as *Spiderman, X-Men, Hellboy,* and *The Punisher* as "sure things" at the box office.

 Scott *OK,* X-Men *and* Spiderman *still work, but maybe we should update the other two to* Fantastic Four *and* The Incredible Hulk.

 Kurt A couple weeks ago, I had the privilege of meeting a superhero face to face.

I'd talked to Gary Hunt a couple of times on the phone but had never had the opportunity to meet him in person. When I found myself in Orlando and realized I was only an hour away from him, I called to see if we could grab a meal. He said yes, and I hopped in my rental car and headed to the Cracker Barrel, our agreed-upon meeting place.

There will certainly never be a movie made about Gary Hunt, but there should be. Gary is a 54-year-old who works full time leading a middle school ministry. He's been doing this junior high ministry thing a long time.

 Scott *Some might guess Kurt's a know-it-all youth pastor from a big church. But he continues to seek out opportunities like this to gain insights from people. Kurt won't like me saying this in his book, but he's one of the most humble learners I know. And Kurt, it sounds like you found a real teacher in this guy Gary.*

Kurt For three hours, Gary poured wisdom and encouragement in my direction while our waitress poured sweet tea. I learned a lot from Gary, and I thought I'd pass along a few things to you.

Stay Focused—Many experts say that to grow as a leader you need to stretch yourself by focusing on what you don't do well. I've always disagreed with this strategy, and Gary's ministry seems to disagree, too. One of Gary's strengths is his ability to build bridges in the community—he spends a large portion of his time coaching at the local middle school, mentoring students on campus, and serving his community in a variety of ways. Because he's good at it and has spent considerable time focusing in this area, he's found success and fulfillment.

What do you do best? I'd encourage you to use the gifts God has given you to the fullest. If you aren't gifted in a particular area, find someone who is and hand over that piece of ministry.

Stay Content—"When are you going to become a real pastor?" You and I have heard that one before. At age 54, just think how many times Gary has heard it! Time and again, Gary has been offered "promotions" that would increase his influence, his leadership platform, his responsibilities, and also his paycheck. Yet because he's content in his calling to minister to young teenagers, these offers, while tempting, have been fairly easy to turn down. I'm not suggesting that it's always a sign of discontent when someone moves from junior high ministry into another area, but it certainly might be.

For most of us, the time will come when we feel God is leading us into a different area. What I learned from hanging out with Gary is that I need to be sure I don't leave for any other reason.

Stay Put—One reason Gary has been able to hang in there for the long haul is because he's stayed put! He's been at his current church for 17 years. Seventeen years of building trust with parents, his pastor, and his community. These people know that Gary could be doing a lot of other things with his skills, and they've come to respect his commitment to middle schoolers. He's had lots of chances to go to bigger churches with larger middle school ministries, but he's decided to stay put.

(Scott) *I'd sure agree with Gary on this one. The first year with a new ministry—or the first few—seems like you're just figuring things out more than you're moving forward. But when people ask me "what I've done" to help our ministry, one of my honest responses is simply that I've stuck around. I remember trying to scare myself with a reality check when I was deciding whether to take this junior high position. I asked my wife, "What if this ministry needs someone to lead it for the next 10 years? Would I take the job?" I'd never done anything for 10 straight years! I didn't know if that's what God would want…but now I'm in my eighth year in my role, and I think staying put is a big part of any ministry success I've seen.*

(Kurt) There will never be a movie about Gary Hunt. But when his life is played before him in heaven, God's going to give him two thumbs up!

What do I think?

Lost in Transition

 It's almost that time—the time each year when junior highers, the same ones who a couple years ago brought their VeggieTales stuffed animals to camp, begin their transition into a whole new world…high school. It's a world of dating, driving, working, college prep, big-time sports, and so much more. It's an exciting time!

 I'll be honest—I hate this time. Three years of memories. I'm not good at goodbyes! Oh, wait…it's not all about me.

 It's also a scary time because it's during the four years of high school that so many students allow the busyness and excitement of life to crowd out the excitement of their faith. Think for a minute. How many times have you looked at the faces in your high school ministry and asked yourself, "What ever happened to so-and-so?"

One of the most important roles of your junior high ministry is to help your students as they make the jump from junior high to high school.

 Even if you lead both junior high and high school ministries at your church, this is crucial!

 Here are a few ideas to keep students from getting lost in transition.

Start early—Begin exposing your eighth-graders to the high school ministry and its leadership several months before graduation. Ask high school leaders to drop by your programs. Ask someone on the high school team to substitute teach for you. Begin "talking up" the high school program.

 Even if you think the high school ministry is a shade less than perfect, you still need to talk it up! Your opinion matters to your eighth-graders…and it can really affect their future.

 Categorize your eighth-graders—Make a list of all your eighth-graders. Who are the leaders? Who's on the fringe? Who needs some extra attention? Who comes from a single-parent home? Answer pertinent questions such as these, and give this list to the high school team to help them begin ministering to students immediately and effectively.

We've used a "profile form" that junior high leaders fill out and pass on to the high school ministry. The danger to avoid is "labeling" a student in a particular way, especially negatively. But helping high school leaders hit the ground running with info is really important.

 Assign a transition "point person"—Ask an adult leader in your junior high ministry to move up to high school for a few months with the students. Ask this person to focus solely on the needs of the freshmen. While I think this is a great role in any size church, it's super-important in a large-church setting. A common complaint among new freshmen is that they don't recognize anyone in the high school ministry. Seeing a familiar face or two each week for a few months helps ease the pain a little.

Do lots of "freshmen only" stuff—During the first few months, look for ways to promote activities for freshmen only. Have high school volunteers show up on these nights to really get to know names and build relationships with their new students.

 Don't miss this great tip! Many high schools really do this well…they know that freshman year will set the tone for the whole high school experience. Or it can serve as a natural exit ramp out of the church! What do you do for freshmen?

 Keep your door open—Be sure to let students know that they're welcome to drop back by the junior high room. In a real way, your room and your team serve as a security blanket—one that students will need to wrap up in from time to time.

 I'll be honest. Keeping the door open probably helps me as much as it helps students. High schoolers remind me that junior highers will be more coherent in a few years…and probably rein in their bodily functions better, too. They also remind me of the future high school pressures I need to be preparing our middle schoolers for today!

What do I think?

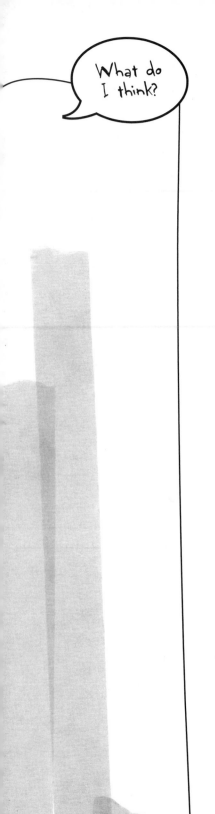

What do I think?

Kurt In junior high ministry, we often don't see the fruit of our work until years later. Sadly, if we don't help our students with their transition into high school, we may not see the fruit at all.

Surprised by the Bible

 Every Tuesday night I lead a small group for seventh-grade guys. It's awesome! We throw around a football, eat great snacks, share prayer requests, talk about life, and work our way through a Bible study. These guys really surprise me.

I'm surprised that they can catch my Elway-like passes.

 Man, I'm holding back several Elway jokes here...

 I'm surprised that they remember to bring snacks on their assigned night. I'm surprised at their willingness to share prayer requests and discuss life issues deeper than whether Xbox is better than PlayStation. I'm surprised at their desire to participate in the Bible study.

I'm also surprised that the only time most of them pick up the Bible is to bring it to small group. I shouldn't be surprised—I've been doing this a long time—but I am.

As junior high workers, one of our most important roles is to help students develop an appreciation for God's Word and a desire to let it impact their daily lives.

 Wow, that last statement is strong...and key! "One of our most important roles"...do you believe that? I do, but does my ministry really reflect that? Hmm...does yours?

 But how do we do that? Let's face it, in today's world of the Internet, blogs, e-mail, instant messaging, cell phones, text messaging, video games, extreme sports, music TV, and movies on command (not to mention the old-fashioned stuff like homework, Little League, and baby-sitting), it's tough to convince a 13-year-old that spending time reading the Bible is actually a worthwhile pursuit.

Here are a few steps I'm taking to help my students value the Bible.

I'm encouraging them to read it: Our ministry has started selling student Bibles below cost, and we give them away to anyone who can't afford one. We've created lots of self-paced Bible studies and devotional guides that make reading the Bible easier. I try to constantly remind our students that "starting small is better than not starting at all."

What do I think?

Scott

Kurt, I'm going to steal that phrase and use it in my ministry. Hope that's OK! Anyone else who likes it has my permission to steal it from you, too. ☺

Kurt

I'm challenging them to remember it: Our small group leaders have been asked to place a higher emphasis on each week's memory verse. We've created Scripture memory incentives. We encourage our leaders to be able to use Scripture from memory as they encourage, counsel, and hang out with their students.

I'm helping them relate to it: Reading and remembering the Bible simply aren't enough. I've met far too many people who've read God's Word and can quote Scripture better than Billy Graham but have still failed to let it impact how they live their lives. When students understand the relevance of God's Word, they'll give it a place of priority. I'm asking more questions that force my guys to relate what they've read to their own real-life situations. I'm giving them plenty of time to ask questions. And when they ask questions, I'm doing a better job of pointing them to Scripture for the answers.

Scott

Read it, remember it, relate to it…great stuff. You're so much better at making stuff all start with the same letter than I am, but I have two more to add:

Help them acquiRe a Bible they can actually read—one that's right for them. *Too many junior highers only have a Bible with more pictures than words, from when they were little…or else a big old intimidating Bible not designed for their reading levels.*

Train them how to navigate their Bible! *Even the simple things can be intimidating when you're getting started. Finding a verse, using a topical index, understanding context…it's like a video game in the sense that if you don't know how it's set up, it'll frustrate you!*

Kurt

I realize my small-group guys may never ask if we can quit playing football a little early so we can get to the business of discussing Scripture…but it would be a nice surprise.

T.H.E. Way to Do Junior High Ministry

 Kurt Stop and think for a few minutes about all that your junior high ministry does: camps, mission trips, fundraisers, Sunday school, small groups, game nights, lock-ins, discipleship, pizza parties, outreach events, service projects, and more. A question I've asked myself quite often is "Are we doing the right stuff?" And there's an even more important follow-up question: "Are we doing the right stuff the right way?" How we do the things we do is, in the long run, more important than the things we do themselves.

Scott *Actually, I think they're both important: the "how" and the "what." And sometimes saying that the "how" is more important can be a cop-out for not changing the "what" we're doing when we need to. Know what I mean? When you look at your calendar, are there any things happening because "we've always done that event"? Or because it's so-and-so's pet project, even though it doesn't make sense to do it anymore? Or because we've not taken the extra effort to think of a new and better thing that will meet needs more? I have to admit it: Sometimes I've waited too long to change the "what" because I'm not courageous enough or disciplined enough to think through a new plan. But after I did make the change, I've often wondered why I waited so long!*

Kurt So I'd like to suggest **T.H.E.** way to do junior high ministry…

Teamwork: By now, most of us recognize the fact that we can't do ministry alone, that it's a team effort. Unfortunately, many ministry teams don't function like a team at all. There are competing agendas, ideas, strategies, and values that often make our team approach to ministry look more like a game of Tug of War.

Teamwork says things such as, "We're all in this together"; "When you win, so do I"; and "We all know our roles and responsibilities." No matter what your junior high ministry does, do it as a team.

Scott *I love to work as a team—don't you?—even though it can seem "less efficient" at moments. I had several new adult leaders on my team this year…and that leadership team didn't know each other well. So we planned an overnight retreat, and the majority of the agenda was just for the team to get to know each other—even though we had a ton of other agenda items that were barking for attention! We told stories of ourselves in junior high and talked about what we love (and don't so much love) about junior highers. It pulled us tighter together and fired up our collective desire to help today's junior highers. Now we're going after those other agenda items…as a team!*

 What do I think?

 Kurt

Humility: Pride ruins things. Ministry is meant to be sacrificial, but sadly, pride often creeps in. Junior high ministry done in humility says things such as, "Everyone is valued equally," "I'll do whatever it takes," and "No job is too small." No matter what your junior high ministry does, do it in humility.

 Scott

Agreed. And I'm proud to say that I'm far more humble than you, Kurt. Wait...oh, man!

 Kurt

Excellence: Not to be confused with perfection, excellence simply means giving God our best effort. Too often we give students second-rate experiences not because we can't do better, but because we procrastinate or rely on our ability to "wing it." An attitude of excellence says things such as, "God deserves my best effort," "Ministry is worth it," and "I'll plan ahead." No matter what your junior high ministry does, do it with excellence.

 Scott

Totally true, Kurt. I remind myself a lot that God gave me his best. And he definitely deserves mine. I think it inspires people, too, as they realize, "Wow, these people really care about this—it must be important!"

Get Out of the Way

Kurt I'm a slow learner…a very slow learner. It's taken me several years to learn this important ministry principle: There are very few things I do in my day-to-day role as a junior high pastor that others couldn't do as well as me or better if I would just give them the freedom to use their gifts. Here are a few recent examples:

Our weekend program: I used to do it all—plan the talks, worry about the videos, choose the games, and buy the prizes. Now a "design team," which includes several volunteers and me, meets once a month to create our upcoming weekend programs.

Our volunteer staff meetings: I used to show up, unlock the doors, throw some Twinkies on the table, and get down to business. Now that I've gotten out of the way, a group of our volunteers creates a theme for each meeting, decorates, and cooks a delicious dinner.

Our spring break missions trip: Don and Karolyn Thompson, two of our volunteers, have transformed a chaotic, unorganized week into what is now the highlight of our ministry year.

In all three situations, the result has been less stress for me, more ownership for our volunteers, and a better program for our students. As a leader I've learned that the times I swallow my pride and trust others to share the load are the times our ministry flourishes.

When you think about it, this is the way God always intended ministry to work. Ephesians 4:11-12 reminds us, "It was he who gave some to be apostles, some to be prophets, some to be evangelists, and some to be pastors and teachers, to prepare God's people for works of service, so that the body of Christ may be built up."

Allow me to give you a free tip: If you want to see your junior high ministry succeed, it's time to prepare God's people for works of service and get out of the way!

Scott *OK, Kurt…I can picture some readers groaning, rolling their eyes, and thinking, "It must be nice to be at a huge church, where volunteers are plentiful, and you have the option to not 'do it all.'" And you know, I think they'd have a point!*

While I think I get what you're saying—that no one can do everything—I do believe that in some situations a youth worker doesn't have any other choice than to be the

What do I think?

jack-of-all-trades! It's great that including other people to use their gifts has lowered your stress level. But what about the people who find themselves leading a youth ministry with no volunteers and high expectations? And how about when you look around and see nobody who's a viable candidate to help you?

We'd probably all admit that there are serious limitations when you're "going it alone." And no matter the size of your church or ministry, running things single-handedly isn't ultimately going to be best for students! So how can you take the next steps?

Visualize the picture in your own mind. What do you need the most help with? Planning talks, getting small group curriculum, playing music, running games, sending communication, leading groups, planning a camp. What drives you crazy? What if you actually had help doing that thing, from someone who was honestly fired up about it? Start praying for that person and looking around for him or her. Sometimes those people are not as far away as we think. Don't eliminate people in your mind too quickly. A person who loves Jesus, whom you get along with, and who has a little bit of ability is all you need to start.

Describe the picture to someone and invite him or her in. We need to cast a vision for what could happen if someone stepped into serving. We're not looking for people who feel "obligated"; we're looking for people who can get fired up about pointing students to Jesus! It's up to us to help them see that their investment can make a difference. A big difference!

Hand them a brush, and let them paint! Sure, they're going to have a learning curve. You did too, didn't you? And if you're like me, part of you may be thinking, "I could do that better (and probably faster) by doing it myself." But in the long run, not only can two do more than one, you're also inviting someone else into the adventure of ministry! So before you decide to run your ministry as the Lone Ranger, think about the picture God might want to paint if you invite a team to do it with you!

Honestly, the ministry I serve has never even had 90 percent of the volunteers we need. So I'm still visualizing, describing, and handing out brushes!

The Parent Trap

 Kurt Early in my ministry career, I was younger, cooler…and a lot more arrogant. I didn't think that I needed kids' parents. After all, they were too old, too conservative, and too, well, too parental! A few harsh lessons and several years later, I've discovered that parents' involvement, influence, and support are crucial.

In our ministry, about one-third of our adult volunteers are parents of junior highers. Parents lead small groups, go to camp with us, help us build houses in Mexico, lend us their Suburbans and summer homes, and so much more. In fact, as I write this sentence, Karen Spain, a parent of one of our eighth-grade girls, is spending her afternoon shopping for our weekend program. We have an unusually high amount of parent support and involvement in our ministry because we've earned their trust.

Here's how you can do the same.

Stick around awhile—Trust is earned over time.

Talk it up—Keep parents informed.

 Scott *Agreed. Without info parents can get pretty upset. E-mail, mail, phone calls…what's your plan?*

 Kurt **Welcome their input**—They're gonna share their opinions with someone; it might as well be you!

 Scott *Yes, but I think there's an "art" to doing this one. It's called Welcoming Their Input Without Making Them Think You're Going to Implement Their Every Suggestion. Parents do have some great ideas (and some not-so-great ones)!*

 Kurt **Act like an adult**—Ouch, that one hurts a little.

Work with them, not against them—Don't undermine their authority with their children.

Be mindful of the "little things"—Return from trips on time, have plenty of release forms, return phone calls, and so on.

When parents trust you, there's almost no limit to the amount of support they'll give your leadership and ministry. At this stage in my ministry, I could tell our

What do I think?

parents that I was going to use their children to smuggle cigars from Cuba, and most of them would say, "Wow, Pastor Kurt, that's a great idea; do you need me to help fund that?" An exaggeration, but you get the point!

Let me encourage you to view parents as your allies, not your enemies. As long as you minister to junior highers, you'll also be ministering to their parents. I hope you'll begin to treasure that opportunity instead of feeling trapped by it.

In our ministry we have a Parents' Weekend every year, where we invite moms and dads to sit in on our ministry and see what we do. When I started doing junior high ministry, my own kids were all preschoolers. During a Parents' Weekend back then, I'd often think to myself, "Well, here's my chance to talk with all these old parents." This year my oldest son is in sixth grade. Last weekend was our Parents' Weekend, and I couldn't believe how young and energetic all those parents looked.

I talk to some youth workers who say, "Nope, we don't have any parents serving in our ministry." And like Kurt says, I think they're missing out! But I'll be honest with you: I think there's a certain type of parent who can serve with students, and a certain type of parent who I'd just as soon see them serve as a greeter at the adult service! Part of our job is to discern which parents have that certain something it takes to work with students and gently redirect any who'd do a better job in a different ministry.

One last thing I'd add about parents: Always pay attention to how their students feel about having them involved. If a junior higher is embarrassed having a parent be a visible part of our ministry, I honor that feeling. Our first priority is the middle schooler's experience, even if it means taking a pass on a great volunteer.

Timeout!

 Kurt I'm a football fan; have been all my life. My favorite team is the Denver Broncos, but I'm really not all that choosy. If there's a football game to be watched, I'm probably watching it.

Scott *Clearly you're not that choosy if your team is the Broncos.* ⌣

 Kurt I like the action, the hard hits, the long passes down the sideline. I really like the creative end-zone dances after a score (except for placekickers…they have no business dancing around like that). In the midst of all the hoopla, one thing stands out to me: the timeout.

The timeout is a fantastic part of football. When things are getting out of control…timeout! When your team has lost momentum…timeout! When the direction is unclear…timeout! When you've been hit hard by the enemy and your vision is a little foggy…timeout! It's in those brief, well-timed moments of rest that coaches hope to re-energize, redirect, remotivate, and refresh their players.

Our lives as junior high workers aren't a whole lot different. Despite our best intentions, things get out of control, we lose our momentum, our direction becomes unclear, and the enemy hits us hard. These things are part of the game… we knew it when we joined the team.

Please hear this: It's OK to call timeout! In fact, it's not just OK, it's crucial. Our heavenly Father is waiting for us to slow down long enough to allow him to re-energize, redirect, remotivate, and refresh our souls.

Heading into a new year is a great time to make timeouts a priority. As you plan your ministry calendar, be sure to schedule some timeouts along the way. Here's a plan I try to follow:

Every day: 20 to 30 minutes
One day a week: Extended timeout (one or two hours)
One day a month: A full day away with God
One week a year: A vacation dedicated to personal renewal

Timeouts are a key to keeping us in the game. Use them regularly, and you may find yourself doing a few end-zone dances of your own!

What do I think?

 Scott *Sticking with your analogy, let me offer another thought. It's not just "personal" timeouts that are important. Team timeouts are equally as critical. You probably call leadership timeouts every now and again, pulling people together to make adjustments. But another thing that teams have going for them is a built-in halftime in every single game. Most of us do some kind of a "ministry kickoff" in the beginning of the year...rallying the troops, casting a vision, setting the course for the year. But I think it's equally important to find a time during the middle of the school year to assess with everyone how things are going. Teams that make good half-time adjustments can come back from an early game deficit or avoid a fourth-quarter collapse. It may be that when you do a halftime assessment, you find that not enough people on your team have been calling their own daily or weekly timeouts as Kurt mentioned above. Or there could be other modifications that need to be made to the game plan. Practically speaking, do you have anything on the calendar during the middle of the school year that can serve as a halftime for your team? Combined with timeouts, that could be a strategy to help your team stay in the game!*

Best-Laid Plans

 Kurt If you were to ask the people around me, most would say that I'm not a terrific planner, and they'd be right—planning doesn't come naturally to me. But around the same time each year (usually the end of the summer), I remind myself of these three important planning strategies.

Plan ahead—Because most of us are sharp-minded, spontaneous, and relational, it's easy to approach much of what we do with a "just wing it" attitude. I propose that no matter how creative you are or how great you are at working under pressure, you'll always be more effective when you've taken the time to plan ahead. Talks are better when they're thought through before you step in front of students. Games work better when you've planned ahead enough to understand the rules yourself before trying to explain them.

What do you want your young people to learn this year?

 Scott *Did you just say "young people"? You're old.*

 Kurt What type of church support do you think your ministry needs? How are you going to recruit more help? These are tough issues. Help yourself out by planning ahead.

 Scott *I'm honestly not a fantastic planner, either. But one thing that really helps me plan ahead is not doing it alone. If I wait until I "get around to" planning, it'll never happen. And when I'm working with a few others who are helping me plan, not only do I come up with a better plan, but it forces me to schedule something, too. For instance, we plan a few months ahead when it comes to the content of our teaching. And I try to never leave that meeting without the next meeting on the calendar. Otherwise by the time I think of it, it'll be too late!*

 Kurt **Plan to change**—Is there a better way for students to register for winter camp? Do we still want to give away WWJD bracelets? Youth ministries are notorious for pointing out the sacred cows in the church while failing to honestly evaluate their own. I'm not suggesting you change just for the sake of change, but I am suggesting that even good things need to be changed from time to time to keep getting better.

What do I think?

 Yep—I think "planning to change" keeps things fresh. One thing we do that helps us make good changes for our more "annual" types of events (camps, retreats, special events, ministry kickoffs, and so on) is to always debrief afterward...and take notes. If I don't have someone write it down, I'll make the same mistake next year when registering students for winter camp! It's like sending myself a file into the future to warn myself of what to do differently. (That's assuming I can remember where I put it.)

Kurt **Plan to fail**—It's going to happen. I don't know when. I don't even know to what degree. But I do know that you will fail at some point this fall...

 ...and probably in the winter, spring, and summer.

Kurt Good for you! I firmly believe that if you're not failing, you're not trying. Risk-takers fail. Sometimes when you plan ahead, the plans fail. Sometimes when you make a change, the change is a flop. It happens. Learn from it and move on!

 I'd also say it's important to know your own personal "risk aversion level" and plan accordingly.

Some people almost never take a risk. They may be the ones who need to push themselves. Other people try to think of a risky way to eat their lunch or brush their teeth...just for entertainment. They may need to ask whether they're taking any stupid risks and keep some accountability in the area of leading students.

Kurt This season's almost over. Relax a little. But someday soon, set aside a bit of time for a planning session.

What Was It Like for You?

 Kurt I absolutely loved junior high school. I can't quite put my finger on why, but those two years stand out as some of the best of my life.

 (Scott) *I always find it interesting that you say this, Kurt, because the majority of junior high workers I talk to would not describe junior high as some of the best years in their lives! But alas, you redeem yourself below.*

 Kurt My favorite bands were Devo and the Bee Gees. An odd mix, I know!

I received a D- in math on my report card. I just couldn't get the hang of fractions.

I went an entire Little League season getting only one hit...a bunt!

I had perfect attendance in seventh grade. This was due solely to the fact that I had a crush on Janelle Farrell.

At a party I slipped off the high dive and landed on my back...about 3 feet away from the pool!

My best friend was Mike Pace. He still is.

I got beat up by a seventh-grader. Unfortunately, this happened when I was in eighth grade.

I set the school record in the 600-meter. I had lots of practice running from seventh-grade bullies!

Obviously, I had my share of mishaps and mistakes. I was squirrelly, obnoxious, and insecure—I didn't always think about the consequences of my actions...in fact, looking back I wonder if I thought at all! But overall, I reflect on my junior high years with a smile. I don't know what your junior high experience was like, but I do know that you had one. And, if you're reading this, I know that you lived through it.

What do
I think?

I imagine that you read books about junior high ministry, that you go to some workshops, and that you network with others in the junior high trenches. I applaud you for taking junior high ministry seriously, but let me ask you one question. It's a question that I believe is just as important as any book you might read or workshop you may attend: What was junior high like for you? Remembering what it was like for you is the best way to start exploring what it's like for your students.

Wait! Before you flip to the next section, take a few minutes to think through what the junior high years were like for you. Look through Kurt's list and make one of your own! Favorite bands, favorite shows, names of friends, most embarrassing moments, biggest accomplishments, crushes you had. Maybe even thumb through your junior high yearbook. When you're done with your list, think about how you felt during those junior high memories. Ever feel insecure? Middle schoolers feel the same thing now. Ever feel really embarrassed? It's still happening in junior highs. Remember the devastation of the first zit? Still happening today. But here's the key question: Did you have an adult to help you navigate it? to listen to your questions? to help you keep perspective on it?

I do this "back in time" mental exercise pretty often. And I lead our junior high volunteers through it at least annually. I did a leader retreat recently where each leader brought a picture of himself or herself from junior high. The point? So we could remember what it was like to be there. It can be easy to think of our adult-sized problems as the ones that matter most. But middle school-sized problems are huge for middle schoolers. And how cool is it that you and I can be there to listen, care, and point them toward Jesus in the middle of it all?

Should I Stay or Should I Go?

Kurt I didn't see it until Thursday morning, but the e-mail had been sent late Wednesday night. It was from a junior high worker who was frustrated and fed up. His junior high midweek program hadn't gone too well, and he felt as though it might be time to quit and move into a different area of ministry. He wondered what he should do. Let me share with you the advice I gave him…

Scott *Oh man, haven't we all been somewhere near there? Maybe not exactly the same situation, but wondering if it's worth it. I've gone to sleep at night sometimes thinking, Am I really doing anything helpful here? I'm betting if you haven't been in that place, you will be.*

Kurt **Pause.** Don't make a hasty decision. Let's face it, games don't always work, lessons aren't always well received, and junior high students are easily bored. Hang in there! The end of a rough junior high event is the worst possible time to evaluate your effectiveness as a leader.

Scott *Not only is it the worst time for you to make that decision, it can be the worst outcome for your students, too. Sometimes a quick decision seems like the best way to cut your losses and move on. But there's a subtle message that gets sent to students when someone leaves…especially when they leave quickly. "One more person bailing out on me…" Pause for your own sake—but pause for theirs, too.*

Kurt **Pray.** I assume you prayed about your decision to begin your ministry to junior highers. I hope you'll do the same before you decide to end it. It may well be that your days of spending your vacation time with a bunch of hygienically challenged seventh-graders is coming to an end, but please don't head for the hills without first hitting your knees!

Scott *Just don't make it one of those 15-second "This-is-what-I'm-gonna-do-just-say-yes-God" prayers. Really pray. And really listen.*

Kurt **Progress.** Once you make up your mind, move forward! If you're going to stay involved, do so with a new sense of purpose, calling, and enthusiasm. If you've decided it's time to move on, be sure to take what you've learned into your next ministry setting. (Word is that senior adults love Chubby Bunny!)

What do I think?

Scott

Sometimes the season after an "almost exit" can be amazing, because it can catalyze some change that you've needed to make for a long time. Maybe you were wiped out because you were trying to do too much yourself; make the move to invite others to help. Maybe you were almost toast because you'd been trying to do too much in your own power; devise a new strategy to ensure you're getting the time alone with God that you need. If you dive back in with the same strategy that put you at the edge of a cliff, you'll end up back at that same edge before too long. What are you going to do differently?

Kurt

Please stay. I know you need to hear God's voice on this one, but I want you to hear mine, too: Please stay! Junior highers desperately need caring adults in their lives, and you just happen to be one. You may be a little frustrated, you may be a little aged—but I hope that you may be willing to stay around a little while longer.

Part of the Process

Kurt

The year was 1980, and I was a middle school student in La Mirada, California. I remember it well. The girls had posters of Shaun Cassidy plastered to their lockers, the Bee Gees were the band of choice, and the Dallas Cowboys were still America's team. However, of all my junior high memories, nothing sticks out in my mind as much as a guy named John Miller.

John was an old guy, 24 or 25, who volunteered as my junior high Sunday school teacher. Every Sunday and Wednesday it was the same thing: three students on a couch listening to John give a lesson that he wasn't prepared to give. To say it was boring would be generous. It didn't matter to me, though, because I wasn't there to hear a lesson—I was there to see John. John was my hero. He took me motorcycle riding. He showed up at my football games. He had a cool van...and a really pretty wife. When I was in junior high, I went to church for one reason, and his name was John Miller.

Scott

Very interesting. I was in middle school at the same time. I agree on Shaun Cassidy, the Dallas Cowboys—all the same. The biggest difference between you and me? No John Miller at my church. Just adults who mostly looked past me...and the few other middle schoolers there. And as a result, we all honestly disliked being there.

Kurt

I was devastated at the end of the eighth grade when John told us that he was moving. After he was gone, I had no desire to become a Christian. In fact, I had no real desire to go to church.

When I did return to church, it was a different church with a different youth leader. The summer before my junior year, the high school pastor at my new church saw me surrender to Christ and get baptized. He saw me become involved in student leadership. He saw me head off to school to prepare for ministry. However, it was John Miller who started the process.

Paul lays out what I call the process principle in 1 Corinthians 3:6-9, and if ever there was a principle that fit junior high ministry this is it—you're responsible to play your part in the process, but the end result is up to God. Not every young person in your junior high or middle school ministry will be ready, willing, or able to make the commitment to Jesus Christ. I wasn't...were you?

So pray for your students. Challenge your students. Give them opportunities for spiritual commitments and growth, but be satisfied with being part of the process.

Here's another perspective to think about: What happens when there is no John Miller in a middle schooler's life? I was getting in serious trouble throughout my middle school years. And while Kurt was surrendering to Christ, I was surrendering to the authorities and heading to juvenile detention. No, no, no…I'm not serious. But as youth leaders, we're trying to do way more than keep kids out of jail anyway, right? Here's what I'm trying to say: When there's no one there to plant a seed of faith in a student's heart, and then to water it and tend to it, the likelihood of it growing decreases. There's a difference between really taking an interest in students (like John did) and just "doing time" with the middle school kids, maybe because no one else will. Junior highers can tell when you're really trying to get to know them, listen to them, love them. Those things will make them forgive a boring lesson or an unprepared class sometimes. We've said it before: Don't underestimate your impact! And when your students become adults, some of them may even think back and point to you as a key reason they're still following Jesus!

And that's even cooler than the Bee Gees.

Shopping for Help

 I spend a fair amount of time talking to junior high youth workers. The conversations vary, but eventually a common theme tends to wind its way into our discussions…volunteers. Specifically, how do we find more of the right kind? I'm not an expert. I do, however, have two hints that may be useful as you "shop" for help in your ministry to junior high students.

1. Know what you want.

Although no two people are alike, and variety is one of God's gifts to mankind, you still need some criteria. Our ministry has a list of seven characteristics we look for in a potential volunteer:

1. Spiritual maturity
2. "Sower mentality" (understands that we don't often see immediate results)
3. Fun
4. Contagious (something about this person should be attractive to young people)

 Nice word choice. At first I thought you were dealing with something else entirely.

 5. Patient
6. Affirming
7. Likes junior highers!

Your list may look different, but the point is this: Do you know what you're looking for?

 I'll add something here. You may even have more than one list, depending on exactly what you're going to be asking the volunteer to do! For our small group leaders, we'd have a list pretty similar to Kurt's seven points above. But not everyone's role in our ministry looks the same. For example, we have a setup team, and they honestly don't have to be very "fun," or even spiritually mature. As long as they have a vision for what we're doing and can move chairs, set up games, and arrange food, they're in! Over time they may morph into a small group leader…or not.

What do I think?

 Kurt

2. Avoid acting on impulse.

Because most junior high ministries are desperate for help, we often act out of impulse, latching onto the first able-bodied churchgoer we can find.

To avoid the temptation, I suggest you set up a system that moves potential volunteers through the following steps:

1. Attend a meeting for potential volunteers.
2. Observe the program in action (while you observe them).
3. Complete an application packet, with references and background check.
4. Interview with the ministry "point person."
5. Begin ministry.

How will a system like this help the most? It allows you to recruit potential volunteers out of impulse, but it doesn't allow you to place them until they've gone through the proper channels.

In 12 years of junior high ministry, I've learned something: It's easier to work hard on the front end to get the right volunteers than it is to work hard on the tail end to remove the wrong ones.

 Scott

This is funny. Here's the comment I had written earlier in the chapter before reading Kurt's last line: "When you're desperate, just remember this: We think it's hard to find volunteers, but it's about seven times more difficult to transition out a volunteer who's really not the right fit!"

There's one crucial thing I'd add to Kurt's five-step system for moving volunteers in. It's a critical step that happens before step 1.

An "exciting" announcement in the church bulletin about the Potential Volunteer Meeting will not guarantee you a room full of great candidates. That's never been my experience. In fact, I've never found the "one surefire way" to recruit middle school ministry volunteers. For us it's always been a combination of about 20 different attempts—announcements in church services, e-mails to parents, personal invitations from you, offering people the chance to "sit in once" to see what happens in your ministry, targeting different ministry areas (like young adults' ministry, men's ministry, college ministry, and so on). The list of recruiting attempts can go on. Some of them work well sometimes but not other times. However, if there's one "best" way that we've found, it's been this: asking our current volunteers whom else they know! There's something in a junior high ministry volunteer's heart that can recognize others who would serve junior highers well. Often the people who are crazy enough, contagious enough, and junior high-friendly enough to be volunteering with you right now...well, they probably have friends who are the kind of people whom you want volunteering in your ministry, too!

What do I think?

Hey People,
Thanks for spending a little time with us,
as we jabbered back and forth!

Clearly, we know way-less-than-everything…
but we sure hope some of this helped.

You know, for me, one of my most helpful "resources" is having
another middle-school ministry lover like Kurt to bounce things
off of. Who do *you* bounce middle-school stuff off of? If there's a chapter
you read in here that you agreed with (or that you thought was kinda
dumb), why not share it with someone else who cares about middle
schoolers? The conversation you have together could spark an idea that
helps your ministry help kids more! And wouldn't *that* be a cool thing?

Keep on caring about those sometimes lovable, sometimes punky,
sometimes just plain ridiculous middle schoolers near you,
and we'll do the same!

Bios

Kurt Kurt Johnston has been in junior high ministry since 1988—and he's still smiling! Currently, he is the Junior High Pastor at Saddleback Church in Southern California. Kurt also likes encouraging other junior high youth workers, and has written a few books and created a ton of resources with that goal in mind. He's also the founder of www.simplyjuniorhigh.com.

He's a rabid Denver Broncos fan and believes orange and blue are God's favorite colors. Kurt spends some of his free time golfing, surfing, and riding dirt bikes. But more than anything else, he likes to hang with his family. He's been married to Rachel since 1991 and together they have two fantastic kids, Kayla and Cole.

Scott *Scott Rubin lives in Chicago, even though he loves tropical weather and there aren't many beaches there. He's the Junior High Pastor at Willow Creek…which is an imperfect-but-still-pretty-cool church. He also loves working with middle schoolers, and trying to help them follow Jesus. He's worked with high school students, too, but for the last eight years he's been a junior high pastor.*

Scott has let junior highers shave his head, bean him with dodge balls, shove horse feed into his face, and he sometimes even lets them beat him in basketball…all in the name of ministry. (When he was in middle school, some of his best friends were named Gumper, Bubba, and Doper.)

Among the biggest honors in his life are being married to Lynette; being dad to Tanner, Dawson, and Brock; and being teammates with his friends at Elevate, the junior high ministry at Willow Creek.

My Playbook

Here's your space to write 10 new strategies you'll add to your ministry's playbook.

1.

2.

3.

4.

5.

6.

7.

8.

9.

10.

My Notes

My Notes

My Notes

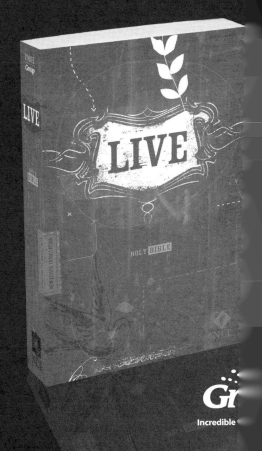

They'll know what to say (and what not to say) as they help others cope with difficult challenges. And they'll be prepared with counseling and care tips, practical advice, Scripture connections, additional resources, and the confidence they need to reach out in love.

+ Emergency Response Handbook for Small Group Leaders
  ISBN 978-0-7644-3181-4

+ Emergency Response Handbook for Youth Ministry
  ISBN 978-0-7644-3574-4

+ Emergency Response Handbook for Small Group Leaders
  ISBN 978-0-7644-3181-4

+ Emergency Response Handbook for Children's Ministry
  ISBN 978-0-7644-3626-0

Quantity discounts available

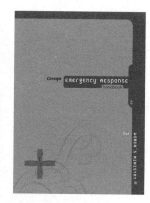